Sandy T.

FRUIT OF THE SPIRIT

By Betty Stevens Tapscott

D1484394

Hunter Ministries Publishing Company
1600 Townhurst
Houston, Texas 77043

Hunter Ministries Publishing Co., Canada
P.O. Box 30222, Station B
Calgary, Alberta, Canada T2M 4P1

The Living Bible, Copyright 1971 by Tyndale House Publishers, Wheaton, Ill. Used by permission. (All scripture verses not otherwise noted are from The Living Bible.)
KJV — King James Version

Library of Congress No. — 78-52276
ISBN No. 0-917726-26-X

Dedicated
with love
to
Gladys and Lloyd Stevens
my
Mother and Dad

Other books written by Betty Stevens Tapscott:

INNER HEALING THROUGH HEALING OF MEMORIES

SET FREE

OUT OF THE VALLEY

INNER HEALING (Pamphlet)

Available at your favorite bookstore or
books, pamphlets, and tapes may be ordered from

Betty & Ed Tapscott
P.O. Box 19827
Houston, Texas 77024

CONTENTS

*"BUT WHEN THE HOLY SPIRIT CON-
TROLS OUR LIVES HE WILL PRO-
DUCE THIS KIND OF FRUIT IN US:
LOVE, JOY, PEACE, PATIENCE,
KINDNESS, GOODNESS, FAITHFUL-
NESS, GENTLENESS, AND SELF-
CONTROL..."*

GALATIANS 5:22,23 TLB

PROLOGUE

e have found in praying with people for inner healing that we often hear this same response: "I'm a Christian, I've asked the Holy Spirit to take control of my life and to fill me to overflowing, but I still don't exemplify the fruit of the Spirit in my life." The questions are asked, "What is wrong? What can I do to have the fruit of the Spirit evident in my life? When I want to be positive in my relationships with others — I'm not. Why am I so negative? How can I change?"

We believe that it is the evil one who comes against us with negative emotions and attitudes to keep us from being more Christlike. We are not just adhering to the old saying, "The devil made me do it." We each are in control of our wills. But we must always realize that Satan *cannot*, and the Lord *will not* override our wills.

The old sin nature of man does enter in, but where does the old sin nature come from? There are two forces in this world — good and evil. If the forces are not good and from God, then obviously, they are evil and come from Satan.

We can be overcomers, however; we can overcome those bad attitudes — those negative emotions. The

Bible in Matthew 18:18 says, *"... whatever you bind on earth is bound in heaven, and whatever you free on earth will be freed in heaven."*

To a degree, we are what we are because of past experiences, either pleasant or unpleasant ones. This is not to put blame or all responsibility on parents, stepparents, or teachers because when we become Christians, we are new creatures in Him. *"When someone becomes a Christian he becomes a brand new person inside. He is not the same any more. A new life has begun!" (II Corinthians 5:17).*

In the books, *Inner Healing Through Healing of Memories* and *Set Free*, we shared how the Lord wants to heal us in our spirit, soul, and body. We shared testimonies of people whom the Lord changed. Praise God that He wants us to be whole. *"... he was wounded and bruised for our sins. He was chastised that we might have peace; he was lashed – and we were healed!" (Isaiah 53:5).* He wants to heal us: spiritually, emotionally, and physically.

Jesus wants to set us free from Satan's bondage. He wants to walk back into our past and heal every hurt, every painful memory. He is the same yesterday, today, and forever (see Hebrews 13:8). The Word in Isaiah 9:4 says, *"... God will break the chains that bind his people and the whip that scourges them ..."* He wants to do spiritual surgery and cut away all the growths of hatred, bitterness, depression, resentment, and unforgiveness.

God loves each of us so much. He loves YOU. You are special to Him, just the way you are. But if you are

not living up to your full potential, God wants to help you be the person He created you to be.

This book is written to encourage each person to try to be that new creature in Him; to be Christlike, to exemplify the fruit of the Spirit. We cannot have the fruit of the Spirit in our lives, however, without first having a personal relationship with Jesus.

1. Do you know Jesus as your Savior? Have you invited Him into your heart? We must each have that real, vital, born-again experience with Jesus. You can have that relationship simply by confessing your sins and by inviting Jesus into your heart (see I John 1:9).

2. The Bible commands us to be filled with the Spirit (Ephesians 5:18). Have you ever asked the Holy Spirit to fill you, and to take control? Have you been willing to let the Holy Spirit *continually* control your life? Have you surrendered every part of your body to the Holy Spirit — your mind, heart, voice, and tongue?

If you have not had that desire to have the fruit of the Spirit exemplified in your life, pray that God will change you. Some people just don't (in the flesh) enjoy being gentle, patient, loving, and kind. They feel it's not worth the effort. You will have to make that decision. "Yes, I want, I *really do want,* more than anything in this world to be filled with the fruit of the Spirit. I really do want to be Christlike."

There is no finer compliment you can be paid than for someone to say, "You're a Christian aren't you? I could tell by the way you acted."

God wants to set us free from every negative emotion. He wants to heal all past hurts. He wants us to be like Him. We should realize, of course, that we'll fail at times. Occasionally we'll "goof," as the young people say. But He wants us to know that He'll be there constantly — loving us, picking us up when we fall, encouraging us when we fail. He'll bind up our wounds. He'll heal our broken hearts. He'll help us take all the bad that happens and make something good. He'll help us learn to make "lemonade" out of the "lemons" that come our way.

God wants others to see Jesus in us in our everyday lives. He wants everyone to see the fruit of the Spirit in our lives.

We need to come before the Lord, humbly, with a broken and contrite heart praying, *"Create in me a new, clean heart, O God, filled with clean thoughts and right desires . . . Don't take your Holy Spirit from me. Restore to me again the joy of your salvation . . ."* *(Psalm 51:10-13).* We can know with assurance that He will hear us — because a broken and contrite heart He will not ignore.

1

BY OUR FRUIT
WE ARE KNOWN

 f someone looked right into our eyes, pointed his finger at us and asked, "Does your life exemplify the fruit of the Spirit?" what would our answer be? "Yes," or "No"? We may be a charter member of the church, attend every service, or serve on several committees; we may be a deacon or a Sunday School teacher; we may even be a minister or music director, and still not exemplify the fruit of the Spirit.

We can *say* that we love Jesus with all our hearts, we can *say* we are filled with the Spirit, and we can *pray* all day long without ceasing; but are we filled with love? Are we really filled with the fruit of the Spirit? This is Christianity in ACTION. By our fruit we are known.

It's a mighty poor advertisement of Christianity when the "agnostic" shows more love, joy, and peace than the "pious" church member. There is no excuse that

will suffice when we don't diligently seek to be filled
with the fruit of the Spirit. We need to have the fruit
of the Spirit not only on Sunday morning from 10 to
12 o'clock, but on Monday morning when it is raining
buckets and the car won't start; on Tuesday when the
phone rings all day long; on Wednesday when the boss
gets angry; on Thursday when we have a flat tire in
5:00 traffic; on Friday when the sales clerk is rude; or
on Saturday when all the family plans go amiss.

That's where Christianity is — in the everyday
"nitty-gritty" living. You may say, "Oh, that's Polly-
anna living." No, it's JESUS living.

Will we always be able to show the fruit of the Spirit
— always, every minute of the day? No, unfortunately,
we won't. Well, perhaps you will be able to, but I
haven't arrived at that place yet. I'm still trying,
though. And that's what God wants. He wants us to
have our eyes on Jesus in such a way that we will
reflect His glory. *". . . we can be mirrors that brightly
reflect the glory of the Lord. And as the Spirit of the
Lord works within us, we become more and more like
him"* (II Corinthians 3:18).

The lady sitting across from me was saying, "Betty, I
can't stand myself; no wonder my husband doesn't love
me as he used to. I know what I *should* be. I know
what I am doing wrong, but I just can't seem to
change. When I want to be loving, I'm critical and
sarcastic. Sometimes when everything is going right and
I should have peace, I don't. At times, I seem to
deliberately pick a fight with my husband. What is
wrong with me?" And without stopping for an answer,
she added, "I'm so impatient with my kids." With that

comment, she threw her hands in the air, completely disgusted with herself. By this time, she was crying, and she ended her tirade with, "Boy, some Christian I am!"

I shared with her that we will not be perfect until Jesus comes, that life is a daily struggle of dying to self, and that just when we think we have a particular problem solved, another old flaw, habit, or attitude creeps in again, and we will have to go through that particular "grade" of learning all over again. We are in "school," and our goal is to become more and more like Him as we press toward our mark.

But we must remember one thing. God loves us just the way we are, and He is concerned (even more than we are) that we become what He wants us to be and what He created us to be. God really does want us to replace all our bad attitudes with positive ones. It is not a one-time job, but a continual process. Inner healing is a progressive endeavor; it isn't a one-time experience, but actually a daily process.

I picked up my Bible and read to her the Scriptures in I Peter 1:2, "... *God the Father chose you long ago and knew you would become his children...*" I read in Galatians 1:15, "... *For even before I was born God had chosen me to be his...*" And Psalm 139:16, "... *You saw me before I was born and scheduled each day of my life before I began to breathe...*"

"Now, do you think God knows all about you?"

Dabbing at her mascara, she said, "Why yes, He does."

"O.K. Now listen to this." And I read what Paul had to say in Romans 7:19, *"When I want to do good, I don't; and when I try not to do wrong, I do it anyway."*

"Why," she said, "that sounds just like me, doesn't it?"

"Believe me," I said, "it sounds like all of us."

But Paul also said in Philippians 1:6, *". . . God who began the good work within you will keep right on helping you grow in his grace until his task within you is finally finished on that day when Jesus Christ returns."*

Then, with a little glimmer of hope, she said, "Oh, do you think I can change? Do you think I can be filled with the fruit of the Spirit?"

My Bible was still opened to the book of Philippians, and I turned to verse 4:13. Handing her the Bible, I said, "I want you to read this Scripture out loud." She read, *"for I can do everything God asks me to with the help of Christ who gives me the strength and power."*

"You mean God will help me to be more loving, gentle, and patient?" she asked.

I flipped over to chapter one of Philippians and my finger slid down the page to this verse, and I read,

> *My prayer for you is that you will overflow more and more with love for others, and at the same time keep on growing in spiritual knowledge and insight, for I want you always to see clearly the difference between right and wrong, and to be inwardly clean, no one*

being able to criticize you from now until our Lord returns. May you always be doing those good, kind things which show that you are a child of God, for this will bring much praise and glory to the Lord (Philippians 1:9-11).

"You know, there is not one thing I can do except pray for you. But I do want you to realize that it is Satan who is coming against you and keeping you from living the Spirit-filled life. You can be set free because *'... greater is he that is in you than he that is in the world'* (see I John 4:4 KJV). Now, I also want to tell you that God will do His part, but you will have to do your part."

We knelt by the sofa and asked Jesus to set her free. We bound Satan from her life in the mighty name of Jesus. I prayed asking the Holy Spirit to reveal all the giants that Satan was sending against her.

Many of the giants she had already mentioned, but there were other negative forces that she was not even aware of. We took authority over the giants of guilt, condemnation, impatience, unworthiness, inferiority, the judgmental spirit, the critical spirit, and the spirit of depression.

We asked Jesus to heal all the hurts that she had suffered. We prayed for her family whom she had hurt. Then we prayed, "Lord Jesus, please fill her with the Holy Spirit and the fruit of the Spirit. Fill the void with Your love, joy, and peace."

It was some time later that I heard from the lady. She said, "Oh, Betty, God has done such a work in me.

He is not finished, though." (I told her we all need to wear the button that says PBPGINFWMY (meaning Please Be Patient, God Is Not Finished With Me Yet.)

She continued enthusiastically, "My husband loves me again. Our marriage is better than it has ever been; but more than that, I like myself. Oh, I still get contrary sometimes, but I know who is making me be that way. It is the devil, and usually, I've opened the door to him by not reading my Bible, by not praying or praising God that day. But gradually I'm a little bit closer to what God wants me to be. Praise His name."

So many times we blame all our problems on our circumstances. "If I'd been loved as a child ..." "If I only could change my looks ..." "If I hadn't married my husband ..." "If we didn't live in this house ..." "If I could get a different job ..." "If we hadn't moved so much, things would be different."

Paul said, "... *I have learned the secret of contentment in every situation* ..." *(Philippians 4:12).* I had a friend who moved fourteen times in seventeen years; she laughed and said, "I really know what Paul means." Malcolm Smith, an anointed Bible teacher said, "There are no 'accidents'; we are where we are because *that is where God wanted us to be!* Everything that happens to us is 'Father-filtered.' "

I want to share with you in this book what my husband Ed calls the replacement concept. That is replacing all the negative thoughts and deeds with positive ones. There was a song when I was growing up entitled, "Accentuate the Positive and Eliminate the

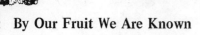

Negative." That is exactly what God wants us to do. He wants us to let the Holy Spirit be in control of our lives. He wants to fill us with the fruit of the Spirit: And —

> "... WHEN THE HOLY SPIRIT CON-
> TROLS OUR LIVES HE WILL PRO-
> DUCE THIS KIND OF FRUIT IN US:
> LOVE,
> JOY,
> PEACE,
> PATIENCE,
> KINDNESS,
> GOODNESS,
> FAITHFULNESS,
> GENTLENESS,
> AND
> SELF-CONTROL ..."
> Galatians 5:22,23

BY OUR FRUIT WE ARE KNOWN —

"LOVE IS VERY PATIENT AND KIND, NEVER JEALOUS OR ENVIOUS, NEVER BOASTFUL OR PROUD, NEVER HAUGHTY OR SELFISH OR RUDE. LOVE DOES NOT DEMAND ITS OWN WAY. IT IS NOT IRRITABLE OR TOUCHY. IT DOES NOT HOLD GRUDGES AND WILL HARDLY EVEN NOTICE WHEN OTHERS DO IT WRONG. IT IS NEVER GLAD ABOUT INJUSTICE, BUT REJOICES WHENEVER TRUTH WINS OUT. IF YOU LOVE SOMEONE YOU WILL BE LOYAL TO HIM NO MATTER WHAT THE COST. YOU WILL ALWAYS BELIEVE IN HIM, ALWAYS EXPECT THE BEST OF HIM, AND ALWAYS STAND YOUR GROUND IN DEFENDING HIM."

I Corinthians 13:4-7

"THERE ARE THREE THINGS THAT REMAIN – FAITH, HOPE, AND LOVE – AND THE GREATEST OF THESE IS LOVE."

I Corinthians 13:13

2

THE FRUIT OF LOVE

he world is hurting today. Many people are lonely; they feel unloved and rejected. I read in the paper of a woman who sent a note to the newspaper stating that she would pay someone to call her and talk to her every day on the telephone. How lonely, how neglected she must have felt to cry out for the voice of a stranger to comfort and befriend her.

There are always those around us who need our love, if we will just reach out to them. Many people are starved for a smile, a friendly hand-shake, a pat on the back, a kind word. All these things we can give as a form of love in action.

Where does love begin? Love begins at home. To get love, we must give love and appreciation. Tell your husband and children every day, "I love you." We have three teen-age children, and I try to tell them everyday that I love them. Our oldest son is away from home now, but every time we see him or talk to him on the phone, I tell him, "I love you." It doesn't have to be "mushy" as the kids say, but go up to your teen-age kids, give them a pat on the shoulder and say, "Hey, I love ya."

One day several years ago, about 5:00 in the afternoon, my little daughter said, "Mother, you know what?"

"No, what?"

"You haven't told me you loved me today." You better believe I did some catching up.

Write or call your parents (and your husband's parents, also); tell them you love them and appreciate them. I appreciate my Christian parents, and I thank God for them. I hear so many negative things about in-laws, but I thank God for my Christian mother-in-law and for my father-in-law who has graduated and gone to celebrate life with God.

Husbands, tell your wives every day that you love them. You may say, "She should know that I love her. I put food on the table, don't I?" Some husbands say, "Well, I'm not good at showing emotion; I'm just like my dad, and he never showed love to my mother, either." That's a lot of nonsense. You *can* show love, and it's imperative that you do so — by actions and words. Show love with your eyes. Hold hands in church. Bring your wife little joy-gifts. It's not the amount of money spent, but the thought that counts.

Many husbands and wives in supposedly solid marriages are crying out in silence because they desperately need love from each other, and it is only their strong spiritual foundation that keeps their marriage together.

We must never take a mate for granted. We must never put the children, church, or business ahead of our mate. As I said before, love begins at home.

We also need to love ourselves. "Love myself? Why, that would be the sin of pride," you might say. No, it is not pride at all. We need to have a good image of ourselves. We need to have self-esteem, self-worth.

If you were always told that you were a failure, that you were no good, that you were ugly, that you were a trouble-maker, you will have a very poor picture of yourself. Your life may become a self-fulfilling prophecy. Because you were told so many times that you were dumb and wouldn't amount to anything, you may discover that you lose one job after another and that you are not successful in anything. You may find that you are incapable of showing love to others. You may find you are not able to receive God's love or return His love.

It is vital that you love yourself, not in a selfish, self-centered way, but as a very special, unique person, created by God Himself. Some may say, "But I was an 'unwanted' baby." Perhaps it's true; you may have been unwanted by your parents, but it was God who gave you life. He wanted and loved you then — and loves you now.

I prayed with a lady one day who said, "I just hate my mother-in-law. She doesn't like me, either. She has never said one kind thing to me in the thirty years my husband and I have been married."

I looked at this beautiful lady so well-dressed, so well-mannered, attractive, with such a pleasing

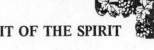

personality, and I thought, "What mother-in-law would not be proud to have her as a daughter-in-law?"

She shared some of the ways during the years that her husband's mother had crushed her with her sharp tongue and unloving spirit.

"Do you know what is wrong with her?" I asked. "She feels inadequate. She feels threatened and rejected. She is still trying to hang on to her son because somewhere in the past, she has been rejected. Your mother-in-law just feels unloved."

The lady said, "You know, you're right. She was rejected by her husband. Do you mean that her haughty spirit all these years has been a cover-up for fear of rejection and loneliness?"

"Yes, I believe that's right."

"Thanksgiving holidays are coming," the lady said, "and I just can't stand the thought of having to spend the holidays with her. I come back home almost sick every time."

"We are going to pray with you for inner healing and ask the Lord to set you free, to heal those hurts, and to mend this relationship."

She was such a lovely Christian woman, but Satan had come against her with resentment, bitterness, unforgiveness, and hatred. But praise the Lord, she renounced those attitudes that morning. We asked Jesus to heal every painful memory of every situation when her mother-in-law had excluded her, lashed out at her, and criticized her.

Then I prayed, "Jesus, please fill this precious woman with Your love, joy, and peace. Lord, stand between this lady and her mother-in-law and let Your divine love flow between them, healing all broken relationships." We interceded in prayer for the "grumpy" mother-in-law, also.

I encouraged the lady to continually forgive her mother-in-law. "I want you to start praying for her. I want you to ask God's blessing on her. Then, when you see her, don't wait for her to act – you act with love and kindness. Go directly to her and put your arms around her and love her. Do all these things as unto Jesus."

During the following year, I heard from this lady several times. The first time was a phone call. She was so excited. "It worked, it worked!" she exclaimed. "I did just what you said, and you know what? I actually found myself loving that mother-in-law. I even enjoyed the holidays. These were the first holidays I have ever enjoyed being with her. Praise the Lord." Several months later, a letter came saying, "I feel so different. God has healed all the hurts in me. I can't praise Him enough."

Then, just recently, she called again to say, "I'm planning my mother-in-law's birthday party, and I can hardly wait for the Thanksgiving and Christmas holidays to do something nice for her." This has truly been a miracle of reconciliation. Praise the Lord.

If you're having trouble showing love, could it be also that you have some unforgiveness in your heart? Is there someone you need to forgive? God's Word says in Matthew 6:14,15 that if we don't forgive, we won't be forgiven. You *cannot* hold unforgiveness in your heart and show love at the same time. Ask the Lord to reveal if there is anyone you haven't forgiven: mate, parent, child, teacher, business partner, friend, neighbor, relative. Resentment and unforgiveness are like poison that will destroy.

It may be that we really can't love God because we are blaming Him for something. God is sovereign. He does no wrong. But sometimes in our own warped emotional make-up, we may need to forgive God. Unforgiveness keeps us from fellowship, not only with God, but also with others.

Recently, a young mother shared that her life had been a series of affairs one after another. In searching for the root cause of the problem, the cause wasn't long in coming to the surface. As a child, she never received love from her dad. He was a very stern, hard, angry man who always pointed his finger in her face when correcting her.

Even though this dad was head of the deacons and held other offices as the pillar of his church, he still could not, or would not, show Christian love to his family at home. Consequently, the daughter grew up feeling rejection, feeling starved for love but seeking for it in all the wrong ways and in the wrong places. Is it any wonder that this young woman had a hard time accepting God's love? Since she had never received love from her dad, she didn't have a foundation on which to base the right kind of love.

The same day we prayed for this young woman who did not receive love from her earthly father, we also prayed with a couple. The husband had been damaged

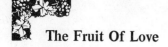
by the possessive love of a mother. Perhaps as damaging as being "unloved" is being "over-loved" with a possessive, manipulative love. Binding emotional ties as these strangle, control, and devour a person. Someone has said that possessive love is a form of witchcraft. It seeks to control another's will by manipulation.

There must be a happy medium in giving and showing love. Christ's love is love without any strings, without conditions.

> Not, "I'll love you if you give me a fur coat, or a new car . . ."
> Not, "I'll love you if you cut your hair."
> Not, "I'll love you if you make straight A's."
> Not, "I'll love you if you go to church."
> Not, "I'll love you if you behave yourself."

Love is *listening,* sharing, understanding, believing, caring, *listening,* laughing together, crying together, *listening.* Love is acceptance — accepting another just the way God accepts us. Love is loving the unlovely; it is loving those who do not love us back. Love is showing appreciation; love is remembering; love is being sincere; love is giving and giving and giving.

If you have an unloving spirit, if you're not demonstrating the fruit of love in your life, if you were unloved as a child or unloved as a husband or wife, if you find it difficult to show love, ask God to fill you with His divine love and to heal all your painful memories. Ask Him to fill the void in your life. You can plant seeds of love if each day you:

> Mend a quarrel,
> Search out a forgotten friend,

Dismiss a suspicion and replace it with trust,
Write a letter to someone who misses you,
Encourage a youth who has lost faith,
Keep a promise,
Forget an old grudge,
Examine your demands on others and vow to
reduce them,
Fight for a principle,
Express your gratitude,
Overcome an old fear,
Take two minutes to appreciate the beauty of
nature,
Tell someone you love him,
Tell him again,
And again,
And again.*

A movie a few years ago ended with the phrase,
"Love is never having to say you're sorry." But Christ's
love is being able to say, "I'm sorry, please forgive;" or,
"I forgive."

*"There are three things that remain — faith, hope,
and love — and the greatest of these is love"* (I
Corinthians 13:13).

*Appeared in the paper anonymously.

PRAYER TO BE FILLED WITH LOVE

Lord, Your Word says for me to love one another, and to love others as myself. First of all, Lord, please help me to love myself as You love me. If I have not always received love from others, please fill that void.

Lord, I pray that You will set me free from any unloving spirit. Take away all unforgiveness and feelings of rejection. Lord, please melt this cold heart of mine. Set me free from my judgmental spirit. Help me to love — the way You love. Help me to love those who may not love me back, who are unloving and unlovely. Help me to love unconditionally.

Lord Jesus, please fill me with Your precious love. May Your love glow on my face, shine from my eyes, and spill forth from my mouth in praises unto You.

And I just want to tell you again, Lord, how much I love You, how much I appreciate You. Please forgive me when I don't show my love to You. It's in the name of Jesus I pray. Amen.

SCRIPTURES ON LOVE

Philippians 1:9 *"My prayer for you is that you will overflow more and more with love for others, and at the same time keep on growing in spiritual knowledge and insight . . ."*

I John 4:7 *"Dear friends, let us practice loving each other, for love comes from God and those who are loving and kind show that they are the children of God, and that they are getting to know him better."*

I John 4:16 *". . . God is love, and anyone who lives in love is living with God and God is living in him."*

I Peter 1:22 *"Now you can have real love for everyone because your souls have been cleansed from selfishness and hatred when you trusted Christ to save you; so see to it that you really do love each other warmly, with all your hearts."*

I John 4:20 *"If anyone says 'I love God,' but keeps on hating his brother, he is a liar . . ."*

Proverbs 17:9 *"Love forgets mistakes; nagging about them parts the best of friends."*

Romans 13:10 *"Love does no wrong to anyone. That's why it fully satisfies all of God's requirements. It is the only law you need."*

Matthew 5:44 *". . . Love your enemies! Pray for those who persecute you!"*

Matthew 22:37-39 *". . . Love the Lord your God with all your heart, soul, and mind. This is the first and greatest commandment. The second most important is similar: 'Love your neighbor as much as you love yourself.' "*

3

THE FRUIT OF JOY

can remember as a little girl that my mother would always say as I went out the front door for school, "Betty, be sure and give everyone a smile today." I praise God for that training, because I grew up "smiling." More than once I've been introduced as the speaker who smiles the entire time she speaks.

The Bible says, *"... the joy of the Lord is your strength" (Nehemiah 8:10).* There have been many times, however, when I've had to sing that song over and over, praying that the confession of my mouth would give me the strength that I needed, because when I got up, I didn't feel joy; I felt *tired!*

We can lose our joy in different ways:

(1) Mental Fatigue: Are we filled with tension and stress? Is our mind boggled with decisions to make? We can lose our joy because we are endeavoring to do more things in twenty-four hours than can be done. Have we

over-extended ourselves? God gives supernatural strength, but He also gives us common sense to have a balance in our lives. (I'm writing to myself, also.)

(2) Spiritual problems: Unconfessed sin and guilt will cause us to lose our joy. There must be repentance, confession, and restitution before we can expect our joy to return. Unforgiveness and resentment toward someone will cause us to lose our joy. We must forgive continually to retain a happy frame of mind.

(3) Physical problems: Physical problems can cause us to lose our joy. Are we in good health? Some bodily disease may be causing the depression. We may need more rest. We abuse our bodies so often by not getting enough rest, or on the other hand, we may need more exercise. We can even feel the "blahs" because we aren't eating correctly — good, nutritional food.

I remember one lady who came for prayer who was convinced that she had lost her salvation, that all her faith was gone, and that the Holy Spirit had left her. It seemed to me that the Lord was saying that she should see a medical doctor, that her problem was physical rather than spiritual. God could have healed her instantly, but He chose to heal her through the doctors. She made her appointment and found out that her despair and depression were caused by a severe kidney infection, an extremely low hormone count, and border-line hypoglycemia. Before long, with medication, she was feeling her old self again, filled with joy.

(4) Adverse circumstances: We can lose our joy by having all sorts of problems crash in on us. When Satan tries to come against us, as he does every chance he

gets, we must do what God's Word says in I Thessalonians 5:16-18, *"Always be joyful. Always keep on praying. No matter what happens, always be thankful, for this is God's will for you who belong to Christ Jesus."* Ephesians 5:20 says, *"Always give thanks for everything to our God and Father in the name of our Lord Jesus Christ."* Some Christians get "bent-out-of-shape" over, do we praise God *in* the circumstances or *for* the circumstances? If Satan can keep us busy "pondering" over the prepositions (in or for) and not praising at all, then that is exactly what he wants. So, WE ARE TO PRAISE GOD — PERIOD!

Especially, are we to praise Him when we feel glum and sad. With authority and expectancy bind the spirit of depression and go through the house praising the Lord. If you say, "I can't think of anything to praise Him for," then sit down with pen and paper and make a list. "And it will surprise you what the Lord has done," is the way the song goes.

One of our most joyous Christmases could have been marred, except for the joy of the Lord.

It was Christmas Eve. I had Christmas breakfast and dinner all ready to pop into the oven the next morning. The table was beautifully set with crystal, china, and silver. The presents were all under the tree. My mother and I were sitting in the living room enjoying the Christmas lights. Suddenly, Mother made a practical suggestion. "Betty, let's do a load of wash since tomorrow is a holiday." So we gathered up a few dirty things, threw them into the washer, and settled back to enjoy the "night before Christmas."

Just a few moments had gone by when one of the kids let out a yell, "Come quick! There's water everywhere!" And sure enough, there was. The washer did something it had never done before. It overflowed — and overflowed — and overflowed. Water was in the utility room, breakfast area, in the edge of the den, and all in the kitchen. It had gone into the dining room (underneath that beautifully set table). The water flowed into the living room under the piano, and just to the edge of the Christmas tree — and those beautifully wrapped presents.

Well! I had been sharing with my mother all about *the joy-of-the-Spirit-filled-life!* And you know, at that moment joy actually did just sweep over me — even in this minor calamity. We quickly got every towel in the house, and the mop buckets — and the entire family started mopping up the mess. We had to move the piano, "unset" the table, move the Christmas presents from under the tree; but we were all singing, "If you want joy, you must 'mop' for it." We were overcome with hilarity. To this day, the kids say, "Remember the Christmas when . . ."

So, in all circumstances, praise Him!

This episode was really just a minor problem. Some people go through severe trials. In I Peter 4:12-13, God says, *"Dear friends, don't be bewildered or surprised when you go through the fiery trials ahead, for this is no strange, unusual thing that is going to happen to you. Instead, be really glad — because these trials will make you partners with Christ in his suffering, and afterwards you will have the wonderful joy of sharing his glory in that coming day when it will be displayed."*

Jack Brewer, founder and director of Boys' Country, a home for homeless boys in Houston, related a story that a hitchhiker shared with him one day. The hitchhiker said, "You know, I am so happy, that when I pick up my right foot, it says, 'Glory' and when I pick up the left, it answers, 'Hallelujah!' "

We shudder to think about living in a country where we would have to wear a badge on our arm or a mark on our forehead. But we ought to be so filled with God's love and joy, that everyone who looks at us knows we are Christians.

If you've been a negative person, grumpy or glum, ask God to replace the negative emotions with His joy. It is actually an affront to Him for us to be grumpy. How unappreciative can we be? We should be joyous for no other reason than for the glorious fact that we have the promise of life eternal.

The kind of joy that God wants us to have is not the "here-one-minute, gone-the-next joy," but the deep, abiding joy and contentment that come only from the Holy Spirit. Your circumstances may not be joyful, but you can depend on the Lord to minister peace and joy to you if you ask for them.

I'm reminded of the father of a dear friend who came for prayer one night. He had a tumorous kidney removed one year earlier. The Lord speeded the healing process beautifully, but he had begun to have pain and discomfort again. As much as he tried not to, he began to think this new pain surely was something very serious.

His daughter drove her father and mother to our home before he had the new X-rays, extensive blood work, and all the tests run again. We visited and had a brief time of prayer asking God to heal and minister to him. The presence of the Lord was so precious. The wife said later, "I could just feel the warmth of the Holy Spirit."

The man shared later what the Lord did that night after he left our home. He said, "I dreamed I was completely well! In my dream, I felt such peace and joy. I woke up after the dream with such a good feeling — all the pain was gone." He went on to say in a letter, "I began to feel and probe myself to see if I were asleep or if I were really awake — but all the pain was gone. I felt so wonderful. I couldn't believe it. I felt such joy."

Later, his tests showed that his blood was fine, his X-rays were fine, and the liver was functioning perfectly! The physical healing was beautiful, and we praise God for it; but we also thank God for His presence and for ministering not only His healing, but also His peace and joy to this precious man — even as he slept.

There is a phony joy that is like cheap tinsel; but there is a joy that comes from the Lord that knows no bounds. At the end of an inner healing service, a tiny young woman came to the front of the church. She waited until almost everyone had left, and she said, "I want you to know the Lord healed me tonight. My circumstances are horrible; my husband is divorcing me." And she named several other problems. She continued, "My numerous problems have just about gotten me down, but I came tonight really expecting the Lord to lift this oppression and to heal me. And He did!" Her face was glowing. I was reminded of Paul and

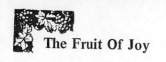

Silas and thought, "Surely, that must have been the way they were in prison – singing and praising God."

I like to believe that Jesus had a sense of humor. I believe He must have enjoyed a good laugh. He was compassionate, loving, and joyful. As Christians, we need to cultivate a sense of humor. We need to be able to laugh at ourselves, and our mistakes.

We can become so "heavenly-minded", that we are no "earthly good." We can become such "pious" sisters of the missionary society, that we turn people away. We must never lose our "humanness," our "down-to-earthness," our joy, our sense of humor.

There is no place for teasing or practical jokes at another's expense; but neither is it much fun to be around those who are always serious, who never smile, who do not have a sense of humor, who are stiff. The Lord wants us to have His joy.

His Word says in John 16:24, ". . . *Ask, using my name, and you will receive, and your cup of joy will overflow.*"

Let's pray for that joy, shall we?

PRAYER TO BE FILLED WITH JOY

Dear Lord, help me to be a happy person. Forgive me for my negativism, for my "grumpy" attitude. Please fill me with joy — even when things go wrong. I pray Your joy will bubble forth from way down deep inside. Help me to be happy, even as old age comes. Make me be the type of person that radiates Your joy.

And Lord, I don't want to wear just a "joy mask," but I want to really feel joy. I pray that You will go to the root cause of my unhappiness and set me free. Please heal all the hurts that the evil one has used to rob me of my joy. Take away all my negative confessions and fill my mouth with positive confessions. I pray You will heal me — spirit, soul, and body. In Jesus' name. Amen.

SCRIPTURES ON JOY

Philippians 4:4 *"Always be full of joy in the Lord; I say it again, rejoice!"*

Nehemiah 8:10 *"... the joy of the Lord is your strength. You must not be dejected and sad!"*

I Thessalonians 5:16-18 *"Always be joyful. Always keep on praying. No matter what happens, always be thankful, for this is God's will for you who belong to Christ Jesus."*

Proverbs 17:22 *"A cheerful heart does good like medicine, but a broken spirit makes one sick."*

Psalm 16:11 *"You have let me experience the joys of life and the exquisite pleasures of your own eternal presence."*

John 16:24 *"... Ask, using my name, and you will receive, and your cup of joy will overflow."*

4

THE FRUIT OF PEACE

 others, we so often set the emotional tone for our household. Is our household peaceful? It may be busy with people coming and going, the phone ringing; but is it basically peaceful? We need to put ourselves in our husband's shoes. Would we actually want to come home and have a barrage of things hit us the way they hit him so many times?

I recall such an afternoon several years ago. It was 5:30, when the front door opened and Ed was home. He took two steps inside the door, and our little daughter said, "Daddy, I need help with my homework." He took another two steps, and one son said, "Hey Dad, my car broke down today, and I need you to help me fix it." The other son walked up and said, "Dad, I need to talk to you; I need some money." By this time, Ed had his tie off, and he walked into the kitchen. There was no kiss from me, just, "Oh! Hi, Honey. Boy, you wouldn't believe today. The phone has rung all day long, the dryer broke . . ." and on and on I spilled out my frustrations of the day. He looked over at the unset table and discovered that dinner wasn't ready. I thought later, "You know, I think if I had been in his shoes, I would have gone back to the office." Men should help keep peace in the home, too.

We had a neighbor once whose husband was a traveling salesman. When he was away, everything was quiet on the home front. The dog didn't bark; the kids didn't fight; all was peaceful. But the moment his car drove into the driveway, within ten minutes you could hear the kids screaming and yelling and the dog chasing the cat. It was just chaos.

When people come to our home for prayer and counseling, they comment on the fact that they can feel the Holy Spirit's presence — that it is so peaceful, so quiet. I would like to say it is that peaceful *all* the time, but it isn't. A good friend has been here many times when it was a three-ring circus, and she has said, "Betty, how can you stand all these things happening at once?"

But our homes need to be havens. We need to strive for them to be havens of peace.*

You may say, "I feel so up-tight on the inside. I feel such inner turmoil, such tension. Not only do we not have peace at home, but there is no peace within me, either. How can I find peace?" Ephesians 2:14 says, *"For Christ himself is our way of peace . . ."* Isaiah 26:3 states, *"He will keep in perfect peace all those who trust in him, whose thoughts turn often to the Lord!"*

*I'm aware there are situations where it is extremely difficult to maintain peace and calmness in the home. This is true especially if there is an alcoholic parent, an autistic child, or an extremely argumentative and abusive mate. Only God can completely calm these storms.

Our only true peace comes through Jesus. It does not come through tranquilizers; it does not come through liquor. Oh, they may both give you a moment's quietness or "numbness," but the source of the unrest is still there.

We have found in our own home that the television at times, has caused such tension and turmoil. Sometimes parents use television as a baby-sitter and allow their children to sit unsupervised in front of the "one-eyed monster," taking in and polluting their minds with garbage.

There are some good educational programs that are worthwhile. However, the "cops and robbers" shows, the loud shows with violence, do not instill peace and calmness in our children. Is it any wonder when the set is turned off, that the young child can't turn off his emotions just as easily? Many times, his emotions have been aroused. He is "hyper," running through the house reenacting the excitement he saw on the screen. And how many times have we read in the newspaper the headlines of a murder, and it was later discovered the murderer got the idea from a horror movie on television!

Keep a supply of library books on hand for your child to read. Cultivate and encourage the use of quiet and peaceful – but fun and educational – games. We can encourage peace and harmony in our homes just by keeping the noise level down and by keeping our voices quiet.

As a teacher, you learn very quickly that you can quiet a noisy, out-of-control class by standing still, by not talking for a moment, and then by speaking just above a whisper. Over and over, we've heard other teachers say that the days they had throat problems and had to speak quietly were the days the children were the best behaved.

How can we get more peace within our homes? How can we feel more peaceful? Do you remember what Jesus did when the storm was raging? He slept. He wants us to have that same kind of peace. Of course, we're going to have "storms" come against us from time to time. When the emotional waves get high at your house, try the following:

(1)   First of all, take authority over the negative forces of tension and nervousness. With the authority you have as a believer in Jesus, say, "Satan, you are bound from me in the name of Jesus." Then pray, "Lord Jesus, I ask You to please fill me with Your peace."

Practice the process of spiritual breathing that Campus Crusade for Christ encourages. Drain or empty your mind of all thoughts that make you jumpy, nervous, or tense. Keep on saying, "Thank You, Jesus, for filling me with Your Spirit and Your peace. I breathe out tension, and I breathe in Your peace. I empty my mind of all worry, all fear, all frustration, all irritation and anger. I am now asking You, Lord Jesus, to fill my heart and mind with Your peace, with Your love, and Your calmness."

(2)   Take a prayer break. When you find you are losing your peace, take time out to touch your Maker. Read your Bible. Read some of the Psalms that are soothing and comforting. Have a prayer partner to pray with you.

(3) It may be that you don't feel peace because you are physically exhausted. Take a ten-minute break, stretching out and relaxing. You may say, "That sounds well and good, but I work. How do I rest in an office?" Take a bathroom or water break and use those few seconds for praying in the Spirit. Sometimes we get into a cycle of tension. Do something to break that cycle.

(4) A great tension-cycle breaker is praise. Just start praising God for the things that are happening; or if you're at work, start to silently praise Him. PRAISE WILL BRING PEACE INTO THE PICTURE.

Several years ago, one of our sons was playing his electric guitar in his bedroom. The amplifier knobs were turned as loud (I think) as they could be. The walls were vibrating, the pictures trembling. I was in the living room reading my Bible and talking to the Lord — trying to commune with God. But that music was really keeping me from being "spiritual." I said — "Lord, that music is so LOUD!"

He said, "Praise Me for it." "For loud, mod music?" I asked. "Yes, for loud, mod music," He replied. So, I said, "Now, Lord, You know the walls are vibrating, the window panes are shaking, the pictures are trembling but I praise and thank You for this music — I praise You, — I really do praise You!" And instantly in the middle of a song, the amplifiers were suddenly turned down and my son started playing the most gorgeous classical piece on his guitar. Praise really works!

(5) We lose our peace sometimes by allowing resentment and unforgiveness to come against us. Every

day we need to do spiritual housecleaning in ourselves
to see if some bad attitude has crept in to rob us of
our peace. Don't allow unforgiveness to have a place in
your life.

(6) Perfectionist wives or husbands can create havoc
in a home. In some homes, children have to leave their
shoes at the door and are barked at for any thing left
out of order. In other homes, husbands leave a list of
things for the wife to do that day, no-matter-what, and
then throw a tirade if she wasn't able to finish it all by
5:00. There cannot be peace in homes like these.

There must be order — divine order (and there are
some closets I *absolutely must* get to). But people who
are perfectionists (never bending) may make life miser-
able for themselves and others.

(7) How do you get peace with toddlers underfoot?
Look, I've been there. I know how hectic it can get
sometimes. But the more we lose control, the more the
children become upset. If that two-year-old keeps hang-
ing onto your dress, whining and crying, then stop what
you're doing and take a "love break" with your child.
Reading one little story may calm the tempest. Hold
her in your lap and love her for ten minutes. (The rest
does both Mom and the child good.) When the kids are
super-energetic, that's the time to put on your thinking
cap and suggest quiet, constructive games.

To have peace in our hearts and keep peace in our
homes, we have to work at and practice peace over and
over again. I can remember that when all our children
were at home, mealtimes often turned out to be the
most nerve-wracking times of the day. Just getting

everybody to the table at one time was a job. Of all times, meal times should be peaceful. I kept saying, "God, help!"

We started trying these things. You might want to try them, too.

(1) During mealtime, take the phone off the hook. At first, I felt so guilty about doing this. But I realized this time with the family was as important or more so than anything else.

(2) Turn off the television. At first there was complaining, but television has done more to disrupt family time than any other thing.

(3) Try eating by candlelight, occasionally. It doesn't have to be fancy special candles. This is a good way to use the leftover Christmas or holiday candles. Moms, be ready for some teasing at first. But you would be amazed how quiet mealtime got.

(4) Pass a rule: "No criticizing." There was a time when as a family, we were together only at mealtimes, so that was the time used to lecture the kids. I'm afraid there are many families guilty of this, too.

A home will never be perfectly quiet and peaceful as long as we have telephones, cats, dogs, friends, neighbors, or children. But think how lonely and uninteresting life would be without all these things. As long as there is life, there is going to be activity, and as long as there is activity, there may be times of unrest, noise, and perhaps even confusion.

Frances Hunter wrote a book called *Hang Loose With Jesus*. And that's what we really have to do to keep our peace in this fast and hectic world we live in today. We have to keep our eyes right on Jesus, because HE IS OUR PEACE. And we have to learn to hang loose.

PRAYER TO BE FILLED WITH PEACE

Lord Jesus, I thank You that You are my source of peace. Lord, help me not to worry about things. Help me to keep my mind stayed on You. Help me to forget the past. Please give me the peace and serenity that I need.

I bind Satan from me in the name of Jesus. I renounce all tension, frustration, anger, resentment, fear, and nervousness in the mighty name of Jesus. Lord, please take all my negative emotions, and fill me with Your precious peace and calmness. Let Your healing power flow through my body. And Jesus, even in the midst of my storms, the large ones and the tiny ones, please help me to remember Your words, "Peace, be still." In Your name I pray. Amen.

SCRIPTURES ON PEACE

Philippians 4:7 *"... His peace will keep your thoughts and your hearts quiet and at rest as you trust in Christ Jesus."*

I Thessalonians 5:23 *"May the God of peace himself make you entirely pure and devoted to God; and may your spirit and soul and body be kept strong and blameless until that day when our Lord Jesus Christ comes back again."*

Ephesians 2:14 *"For Christ himself is our way of peace ..."*

Isaiah 26:3 *"He will keep in perfect peace all those who trust in him, whose thoughts turn often to the Lord!"*

John 14:27 *"I'm leaving you with a gift — peace of mind and heart! And the peace I give isn't fragile like the peace the world gives. So don't be troubled or afraid."*

Colossians 3:15 *"Let the peace of heart which comes from Christ be always present in your hearts and lives, for this is your responsibility and privilege as members of his body. And always be thankful."*

5

THE FRUIT OF PATIENCE

here are no nagging wives, just procrastinating husbands!" The first time I heard that statement, I thought, "Well, praise the Lord! That shifts some of the blame . . . a little." But we ladies are guilty sometimes of becoming so impatient with our children or our husbands, those we love the most. The Bible tells us in Ephesians 4:2, *". . . Be patient with each other, making allowance for each other's faults because of your love."* Psalm 37:7 says, *"Rest in the Lord; wait patiently for him to act . . ."*

We need to listen to our voices, especially when trying to get children off to school. "Will you *please* hurry up? You're *always* late. Did you brush your teeth? HURRY UP! Why are you *always* late?" On and on we go. How would we feel if someone treated us this way? Now, I know we as mothers must remind and discipline our children, but so often it isn't *what* we say, but the *way* we say it. Before we lash out at our children, we should pass a rule that first we pray in the Spirit.

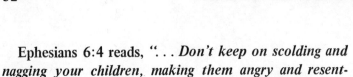

Ephesians 6:4 reads, *". . . Don't keep on scolding and nagging your children, making them angry and resentful. Rather, bring them up with the loving discipline the Lord himself approves, with suggestions and godly advice."*

I think sometimes we become impatient because we may be at fault for some reason. If that child is not ready for school, is it because we did not get up in time ourselves? If we are running late on Sunday morning, is it because as parents, we did not do the Saturday night duties in order to be prepared for Sunday morning? Do we become impatient with members of the family who dress more slowly than we do?

There are some husbands who offer no help in the house or with the children, and yet expect everything done when they say so. They become most impatient when things are not accomplished on schedule. We had a neighbor once who would go out to his car on Sunday morning at 8:30 sharp and start honking the horn until his wife finally came struggling out the door — with a baby in one arm, a big diaper bag over the shoulder, purse and Bible underneath the baby, and with a two-year-old tagging along behind.

"I'm sure it entered her mind, as it did ours, "If only that 'impatient husband' would just help a little!" If every husband had to keep house and take care of the children just for one week by himself, what a difference it would make in husband-wife relationships!

And I must add, if we wives had to work in that big downtown office for one day — fighting traffic, making crucial decisions, meeting deadlines, being responsible for a certain amount of work output we, perhaps, would be a little more patient with our weary husbands at 6:00 in the evening.

In observing parents walking in the shopping center with little children, we often hear, "Hurry up; will you p-l-e-a-s-e hurry up!" The little fellow tries to take bigger steps. Then the parent grabs his little arm, pulling him along. To the observer, it looks as if his little arm is being pulled out of its socket in the process. If we'd only treat our children the way we prefer to be treated by our peers!

It's so easy to become impatient with someone who is falling behind in his spiritual life. We think he should just "shape up," read the Bible more, listen to more tapes, devour more books. We must never forget that someone had to have patience with us when we were first trying our wobbly spiritual legs. Perhaps we have trouble making decisions. Do we become impatient with others who have the same problem?

Another area that takes supernatural patience is living with someone who is emotionally ill or senile. So many times they appear completely normal, and yet the next moment, they exhibit irrational behavior. Our first response may be one of impatience. But of all people, they need our patience and tolerance the most.

So many times we have heard parents of mentally retarded children share how much they (the parents) have grown spiritually. God had given them the fruit of the Spirit — patience, most of all — because of that "special" child being in their home.

Patience is a learned trait. The moment you feel yourself becoming impatient, start praising the Lord for the situation. Take your Bible or a good book or box of stationery with you when you are waiting for your children in the dentist's office or at their piano lesson. Use this time to get alone with the Lord.

When you don't make it through a light before it turns red, just replace that sudden burst of impatience with a great big, "Thank You, Lord; and I praise You." Use that time to pray for people around you who are waiting for the light to change.

Impatience is blaming God. It's believing something is amiss and that God is not in control. When we become angry and impatient, we are saying, "God, You goofed." But beloved, God does not make mistakes.

Recently, my husband's car needed some repairs. This meant I had to get up early one very cold morning, drive my car and follow him to the car repair center. I was beginning to feel a little "put upon." But I should have known that God had something in store. As I waited for Ed to register his car for service, I saw a lady waving her arm and coming toward me. It was someone I had prayed with two years earlier. In fact, she was the nurse anesthetist I shared about in *Set Free.* She was having her car worked on also. She said, "I have been wanting to reach you." We had a delightful time of sharing and praying in the car as I waited "patiently" for Ed to finish.

In today's society, we spend so much time driving — a probable time and place for impatience. Keep Christian tapes in your car, and use the time on the freeway to listen to Christian music. And remember, *praise will push impatience out of the picture.*

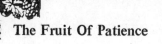

Are you impatient? Perhaps your impatience stems from the way you were treated as a child. A child raised in a home where he was not taught patience, where the fruit of patience was not easily observed in his parents, may grow up being impatient himself. It is especially damaging to a child with a "perfectionist" type mother — one who wants things done instantly and perfectly and becomes impatient and critical if the child is not able to meet her expectations. The child always feels "rushed" and perhaps fearful of not measuring up.

Quick-tempered and impatient people are unpleasant to be around. They always give you the feeling that they are displeased with you, and they tend to make you feel inadequate. Impatience probably compares with nervousness in reasons why people smoke.

I believe the Lord allows situations to come into our path that will strengthen us. The morning my second book, *Set Free,* was to be delivered to the publisher, I tucked the manuscript under my arm, my heart just soaring with thanksgiving: "It's finished! Praise the Lord, it's finished!" I went joyfully out to the car, got in, turned the key, and — nothing — absolutely nothing. Would you believe, the car would not start? It was so obviously an attack from the devil, that it was funny.

I praised the Lord as the service station attendant came and tried to start the car and couldn't. I praised the Lord when he came back with the wrecker and towed the car away. I was still praising Him when we were finally able to take the book late that afternoon and were detained by five o'clock traffic plus a long train. All of these little irritating things could have ruined the whole day. Now, I'm not saying that I'm always "that" patient, but on that day, I was able to practice praising the Lord and it worked!

Perhaps you've seen the prayer plaque that reads, "Lord, I want patience, and give it to me NOW!" I'm afraid He won't listen to that type of prayer. We also need to be aware when we pray for patience that we're going to have many opportunities to grow and grow and grow. So just be prepared, and do remember to thank Him for those blessings disguised as problems, that come to teach us patience.

We've all had our moments of feeling pressed for time, of being impatient. Let's each pray the following prayer to be set free from impatience.

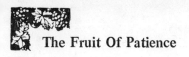

PRAYER FOR PATIENCE

Lord, please forgive me when I've been impatient. And I must be honest, Lord, there even have been times when I have been impatient with You and I ask Your forgiveness. Please set me free from this spirit of impatience, and fill me with Your divine patience. Help me to be more understanding of others.

And Lord, if I am impatient today because I was always "rushed" as a child or I sensed my family's impatience, I ask that You would heal those hurts, those painful memories, those memories I have of feeling slow and dumb. And Lord, please help me to be patient with myself. Help me to always wait patiently – even for Your answers to my prayers.

In the name of Jesus I pray. Amen.

P.S. And Lord, thank You so much for always being patient with me. I Love You.

SCRIPTURES ON PATIENCE

Ephesians 4:2 *". . . Be patient with each other, making allowance for each other's faults because of your love."*

Psalm 37:7 *"Rest in the Lord; wait patiently for him to act . . ."*

James 1:19 KJV *". . . let every man be swift to hear, slow to speak, slow to wrath."*

Psalm 40:1,2 *"I waited patiently for God to help me; then he listened and heard my cry. He lifted me out of the pit of despair . . ."*

Romans 12:12 *". . . Be patient in trouble, and prayerful always."*

II Peter 1:6 *". . . learn to put aside your own desires so that you will become patient and godly, gladly letting God have his way with you."*

Isaiah 40:31 *"But they that wait upon the Lord shall renew their strength. They shall mount up with wings like eagles; they shall run and not be weary; they shall walk and not faint."*

Psalm 27:14 *"Don't be impatient. Wait for the Lord, and he will come and save you! Be brave, stouthearted and courageous. Yes, wait and he will help you."*

6

THE FRUIT OF KINDNESS

here is a book entitled *Try Giving Yourself Away* by David Dunn. He says to show kindness every day by giving ourselves away, by doing little things for others:

> sending birthday cards
> sending "thinking of you" notes
> giving joy gifts
> baking cookies and sharing them with others
> taking the new neighbor a cake or cup-cakes
> making a phone call to say, "I'm praying for you"
> taking food to a sick neighbor.

But he admonishes, don't keep record, and don't expect to be repaid by that person. You are planting seeds of kindness, and God will return them.

How kind are we? How kind are we to the sales clerk, the garbage man, the salesman at the door? We may be the only Christian they will meet that day. How do we measure up? Can they tell by our kind words and actions that we are Christians?

Sometimes when we think no one knows us, we feel we don't have to be quite as "spiritual." But we must remember that our actions are being watched every day. Recently, we had to buy a new sofa. It had been promised as a before-Christmas delivery. That date came and went; weeks went by. My phone calls of inquiry to the shipping department for an expected delivery date were not returned. The sales person who ordered the sofa for us was either "out," or for some reason, didn't return our phone calls. It seemed the thing to do was to call the manager and see if he could help.

Now, way inside, I felt a little agitation. But praise the Lord, I explained the situation to the manager — kindly and with *patience* — and asked his help. When I gave my name, he said, "Oh, are you the Betty and Ed Tapscott who wrote the book, *Inner Healing?*"

I paused and then said, "Why, yes."

"Well," he said, "my wife and I go to the same church you go to!"

Thank You, Lord, for giving me the grace to be patient and kind. We just never know, do we?

A husband may be so kind and "spiritual" to the men in the Christian business groups, but go home and yell, gripe, and even curse at his wife. He may be so sensitive to others' needs and listen attentatively, but his wife may never have a chance to share with him

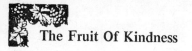

about her own deep needs. Consider the wife who may be such a "pious" person in the prayer group but becomes a nag at home.

How kind are we to our older relatives? Are we unconcerned or impatient? Do we take the time to just listen to them? Sometimes we are more kind to a total stranger than we are to those in our own family. Are we kind to our children? And what about our children's friends?

Have you ever observed two teen-age friends who were so kind to each other until another friend comes on the scene? Then one friend drops little "digs," comes forth with a touch of sarcasm, puts down the first friend, and then tops it off by sharing something to the newcomer that had just been shared in confidence. (Grown men and women play this same game, too.) This is where the test of true kindness comes in. We need to treat others the way we would like to be treated.

When someone looks nice, we should tell her so. When a person does an exceptionally good job, drop him a note saying that you appreciated the job he did. Several months ago, some friends sent me a copy of our son's picture that had been in the paper. I appreciated their thoughtfulness so much. It was so kind of the teacher who took the time to write on her Christmas note to us that she had appreciated having another of our sons in her class.

It warmed my heart when a neighbor called one time to say, "I just want you to know that your young daughter is a little peace-maker in the entire neighborhood." All of these different acts of kindness blessed me and "made my day." I still get a warm glow when I think about it.

I was writing this portion on kindness when a friend stopped by. I asked her what kindness meant to her. She had just been fighting the freeway traffic, and she said emphatically, "Tell people to be *kind* on the freeway and to drive courteously."

And you know, it really is fun to practice good manners in driving. Not only is it a safety feature, but it also makes you feel better, yourself, to let that other person pull in front of you into your lane of traffic. And as an added measure, silently say, "God, bless her."

How kind are we when a car stalls in front of us? Do we honk impatiently? Do we pull out and around the frustrated driver with a "Why don't you learn how to drive?" look. Or do we give him a smile that says, "I'm sorry you are having trouble," and then pray that the Lord will help him get the car started. When it is raining and you are taking your child to school, call and offer to take the neighbor's child to school, also.

Just recently, I hurriedly ran into a discount store to pick up only two items (I thought) and so didn't get a basket. But as I went down the aisles hunting the needed products, I saw several other things that were needed, also. As I made my way to the check-out counter with about six things stacked in my arms, a box of envelopes slid off the stack. I bent down to pick it up, and the tube of tooth paste fell out of my arms. It seemed I was all thumbs all of a sudden and was about to drop everything in my arms.

I stood up to regroup the items, and before I could pick up the two items off the floor, a young man walked up, almost stepped on the items, and walked by without offering help. (I certainly didn't expect it, but it was obvious when he did not offer.) A very well-dressed lady stepped over the two items with a look of "I never dropped anything in my life."

And then, from two rows away, a little gray-haired grandmother came out of her way and without saying, "Can I help you?" just bent down and handed me the dropped items. When I profusely thanked her, she said, "Oh, I always help everybody anytime I can." That's *kindness in action*.

We live in such a fast pace today that we aren't taking the time to be kind. I heard of a pastor's wife who said that in their church, people were so busy going to meetings and listening to tapes, it was hard to find anyone who would take food to the sick, to the person with a new baby, or to the family who was bereaved.

We are usually filled with such good intentions, but then we start reasoning, "What should I do? What can I say? I don't know what to write. I don't have the right kind of stationery. They would think I was a nut if I called and said I was praying for them."

It won't always be easy, and your act of kindness may be rebuffed. I recall many years ago, I took a cake over to a new neighbor from another state. I was met with suspicion and was not invited in. She was not a Christian, but she later accepted Jesus. Who knows? Perhaps that cake taken in Christian love was one of the first seeds planted.

My mother gave me a strong foundation in giving myself away. I can't imagine how many greeting cards she has sent out during the years, or how many joy gifts she has given away. My little grandmother, before she died at 86, had her own vegetable garden and kept all her friends and family in fresh vegetables. Friends hardly ever leave Ed's mother's home without a "start" of some new plant or something she has hand-made. When you are able to show kindness, it blesses you as much as the person who receives it.

There's a glow that comes in your heart when someone is kind to you: when you think back to the special cards, the joy gifts, the fancy birthday cakes baked by friends, the offers to keep your child, and the week-end trips to a friend's farm or cabin.

I think one of the kindest things I've ever seen was a gift I received last Christmas. A friend gave me twelve index cards. On each card was a note: "January — good for one S.O.S. from Betty." "February — good for one big household job." "March — good for one sewing job." On and on they went. Even though we were not able to use all the cards, the kindness expressed in them was so precious. (I wonder if those cards are still good this next year?)

There is a song that says, "What the world needs now is love, sweet love." Kindness is love in action.

We have heard people say, "I was not treated with kindness when I was growing up, so I don't know how to be sensitive to another's needs;" or, "I tried to be kind, and I was embarrassed and hurt." God wants to replace those painful memories in your past. He wants to fill the void with His love. Each day ask Him, "What can I do for someone else this day?"

And remember, this is not just for women. The author of the book I mentioned was a man. Those acts of kindness apply at the office as well. Children are never too young to be taught, "Be ye kind, one to another." I recall a friend who taught her young children to write their grandparents every week and to hand-make gifts for friends on special occasions. What priceless training they were receiving. They were learning first-hand that it is more blessed to give than to receive.

Kindness with a capital "K" is having friends type book manuscripts and proof-read those same pages over and over again with love and patience.

A man who shows more kindness to people than almost anyone I know, is a Spirit-filled Methodist. In his line of work, he comes in contact with people who have just had accidents. He gives his faith away in encouragement and kind deeds. He frequently gives away joy gifts to friends, and he gives to others as the Lord gives to him. No one may ever know the lives he has touched.

Marjorie Holmes verbalized a prayer:

"Bring Us Together"

Oh, God, we go through life so lonely, needing what other people can give us, yet ashamed to show that need.

And other people go through life so lonely, hungering for what it would be such a joy for us to give.

Dear God, please bring us together, the people who need each other, who

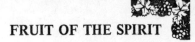

can help each other, and would so enjoy
each other.*

Everyone wants, needs, craves kindness — in words
and deeds. Everything we do should be done in kindness — reprimanding a child or student, correcting an
employee. As the song says, "... a spoonful of sugar
makes the medicine go down ..." The world is starving
for kindness. Let it begin in us.

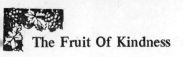

PRAYER FOR THE FRUIT OF KINDNESS

Lord Jesus, forgive me when I wasn't kind, when I didn't give that cup of cold water in Your name, when I was curt. Help me to be aware of others' needs. Help me to be sensitive to others. Remind me, Lord, to be gentle and kind.

Show me ways, Lord, that I can show kindness, and nudge me to take the time to do those acts of kindness. Help me to do good deeds, not just for the friends who return the kindness twice over, but to plant seeds of kindness for a stranger, or for that one who may not even say "thank you." And, Lord, I don't want to be kind just to those I want to impress, but help me to be especially kind to my children and my family.

Please, Lord, heal any painful memory of not being treated kindly. And please fill me with Your love, gentleness, kindness, and compassion. It is in Your precious name I pray. Amen.

SCRIPTURES ON KINDNESS

II Peter 1:2,3 *"Do you want more and more of God's kindness and peace? Then learn to know him better and better. For as you know him better, he will give you, through his great power, everything you need for living a truly good life . . ."*

Ephesians 4:31,32 *"Stop being mean, bad-tempered and angry. Quarreling, harsh words, and dislike of others should have no place in your lives. Instead, be kind to each other, tender-hearted, forgiving one another, just as God has forgiven you because you belong to Christ."*

Colossians 3:19 *"And you husbands must be loving and kind to your wives and not bitter against them, nor harsh."*

Hebrews 13:2 *"Don't forget to be kind to strangers, for some who have done this have entertained angels without realizing it!"*

Proverbs 31:26 *"When she speaks, her words are wise, and kindness is the rule for everything she says."*

7

THE FRUIT OF GOODNESS

f anyone asked us if we were "good," almost every person would say, "Why yes, of course I am. I don't kick the dog or cat, don't hit my wife. Yes, I am a 'good' person."

"To be like Jesus, to be like Jesus, all I want is to be like Him," is the way the little song goes. But are we like Him? Could someone say to you concerning your spiritual inheritance, "I know whose child you are; you look just like your daddy — your Heavenly Father."

Are we really filled with the fruit of goodness? When thinking of this fruit, I think of a clean mouth, clean thoughts, a clean life. Would we be willing to have all our thoughts projected on a screen for all the world to see?

We wouldn't dream of eating food out of the garbage can. We think how foolish even to consider something so outrageous. And, of course, we wouldn't dare give our children food that was spoiled.

But we often blithely go our way, thinking nothing about the mental and emotional food that we put in our minds, or allow our children to digest.

The old health adage, "You are what you eat," applies to our minds. We are what we allow to be put into our computer-like mind.

We need to censor very carefully the books we read, the television shows we watch or the movies we see. This is very important for each of us in the family.

The Psalmist wrote, *"Create in me a new, clean heart, O God, filled with clean thoughts and right desires" (Psalm 51:10).*

The moment Satan tries to plant a negative thought in your mind, immediately jerk that seed from the fertile soil of your mind and instead, plant a seed of praise and prayer.

The old adage, "We can't keep the birds from flying over our heads, but we can keep them from nesting there," applies also to our thoughts. A negative thought may pop into our minds, but we certainly don't have to let it stay there.

Whenever he can, Satan will send feelings of unworthiness, guilt, and condemnation against us. But praise God, there is no condemnation in Jesus (see Romans 8:1). Sometimes we get discouraged and say, "I can never be good enough. I'm not good enough to witness for Jesus. I'm not perfect, so I can't share the plan of salvation. I can't pray for the sick, because I am sick."

Rev. Don Bartow, a Presbyterian minister who was ill, asked the Lord if he should go ahead and pray for the sick. He felt the Lord impressed him that yes, we can share the perfect plan of salvation even though we ourselves are not perfect. We can share God's healing power even though we may be sick. We can never be perfect. We are only a "channel" of God's perfect power and blessings.

Everyday we have choices to make — to be bad or good, to have clean thoughts or impure thoughts. God didn't say we weren't going to be tempted. Our promise is that He will be with us when we are tempted and will not allow us to be tempted more than we can stand.

Perhaps some people are just naturally good. But most of us have to fight the devil all the time. Anything worth-while is not usually acquired without work and effort. We can never become perfect, and we certainly don't want to be a "Holy Joe" or a "Goody-Goody-Two-Shoes." But we must keep striving to become more Christlike. Here are some things we can do to help us become more like Jesus:

1. Read God's Word, the Bible, daily.
2. Pray without ceasing. Just talk with God as you would your dearest friend.
3. Stay in a Christian fellowship. Meet with other Christians regularly. Take time to share your joys and needs, as well as listen and pray as they share theirs.
4. Keep away from places of spiritual darkness, places that would cause you to take your eyes off Jesus.
5. Choose your friends and the company you keep carefully. We are known by our friends and the

company we keep. It is especially important for young people to choose Christian friends.

We pick up the traits of those we associate with the most. If we spend our time with Jesus, we become more like Him. If we spend our time with friends who have bad habits, we will become like them and pick up their bad habits.

Have you ever heard a teen-ager ask, "Why should I even try to be good? I didn't cheat and made a 'C,' and the kids who cheated made a 'B.' " Or what about the man who doesn't know the word *goodness;* he pads his expense account, lies to his business clients, cheats the government, and yet he has it made (money, new cars and success). There will come a day, though, when God will balance the accounts. All those evil deeds do not go unnoticed by God.

Dr. Clyde Naramore related the story of a very successful teacher who used memeographed sheets with the lists of her students' names, and every day she put a check mark by each student's name when she gave him a compliment or praised him. The teacher said that she didn't let the day end without praising or saying something good about each child. No matter how hard we have to look, we can usually find something good in each person. She said that praising accomplished more than anything else.

We are not talking about vain flattery, but sincere appreciation, whether it's for a wife, husband, child, employee or employer. Even the dog knows when he is being praised for being good. There is an empty place in each of us that wants to be appreciated, recognized and encouraged. We usually want to be around those people who see good in us, who bring out the goodness in us. We find ourselves avoiding those who do not accept us, who bring out the bad in us.

In counseling with people who are emotionally ill, we have discovered so often that they cannot find good in anyone. They cannot say "thank you" for gifts; they seem unable to show appreciation. They seem to focus their eyes on themselves and their problem and how bad it is. People who are well adjusted can see good and can compliment others honestly and freely. Have you ever noticed that some people find it hard to say something nice about a friend's new dress, new hairdo, or a man's new suit or what a good job he has just done? An insecure boss is one who never sees the good in his employees, who is constantly critical and caustic.

We use the term "good" so freely. We say, "He's a good student, a good driver; or she's a good mother; it was a good meal, a good ball game." God's Word admonishes us to be good .

Jesus said, "... *Do good to those who hate you. Pray for the happiness of those who curse you; implore God's blessing on those who hurt you" (Luke 6:27,28).*

He continued with, '*A good man produces good deeds from a good heart. And an evil man produces evil deeds from his hidden wickedness. Whatever is in the heart overflows into speech" (Luke 6:45).*

Do we try to see the good in others?

> There is so much good in the worst of us, and so much bad in the best of us —
> That it hardly behooves any of us to talk about the rest of us.

> Anonymous

PRAYER FOR THE FRUIT OF GOODNESS

"Search me, O God, and know my heart; test my thoughts. Point out anything you find in me that makes you sad, and lead me along the path of everlasting life."*

Lord Jesus, I come before You as a little child. I want to be filled with Your goodness. Renew my mind, Lord. Fill me with clean thoughts and desires.

And Lord, forgive me when I abuse this temple of Yours by putting in it things which are harmful.

I don't ever want to feel holier than my neighbor, Lord, but please make me holy. Please fill me with Your goodness. And Jesus, help me see something good in everyone. Help me be the type of person that brings out the good in others.

It's in Your name I pray. Amen.

*Psalm 139:23 TLB

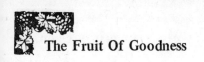

SCRIPTURES ON GOODNESS

Psalm 139:23 *"Search me, O God, and know my heart; test my thoughts. Point out anything you find in me that makes you sad, and lead me along the path of everlasting life."*

Psalm 51:10 *"Create in me a new, clean heart, O God, filled with clean thoughts and right desires."*

I Peter 2:1 *"So get rid of your feelings of hatred. Don't just pretend to be good! Be done with dishonesty and jealousy and talking about others behind their backs."*

Philippians 4:8 *". . . Fix your thoughts on what is true and good and right. Think about things that are pure and lovely, and dwell on the fine, good things in others. Think about all you can praise God for and be glad about."*

Luke 6:45 *"A good man produces good deeds from a good heart. And an evil man produces evil deeds from his hidden wickedness. Whatever is in the heart overflows into speech."*

Ephesians 5:8,9 *"For though once your heart was full of darkness, now it is full of light from the Lord, and your behavior should show it! Because of this light within you, you should do only what is good and right and true."*

Proverbs 11:18 *"The evil man gets rich for the moment, but the good man's reward lasts forever."*

Psalm 11:7 *"For God is good, and he loves goodness; the godly shall see his face."*

Proverbs 22:1 KJV *"A good name is rather to be chosen than great riches, and loving favour rather than silver and gold."*

8

THE FRUIT OF FAITHFULNESS

 aith and faithfulness are almost interchangeable. I heard a man say on the radio, "Faith can only be measured by our adversities." It is easy for us to have faith when things are going smoothly. But how much faith do we have when we lose a loved one, when our business fails, our marriage crumbles, or a child drifts from the Lord? How much faith do we have when we are sick and the Lord doesn't heal us immediately?"

"Where" is our faith? "What" is it in? Is it in God, or is our faith in something else such as:

a certain ministry

a particular person who prays for the sick

binding and loosing

anointing with oil

ourselves

our mate

We must have faith in each of the above things, but primarily, our faith has to be in God. Mrs. Billy

Graham was quoted as saying, "Some wives expect their husbands to be to them what only God can be." We can't get by on our parents' faith. Their faithfulness will not suffice for us.

Can God have faith in us? Are we dependable? Can He depend on us to be faithful and share Jesus to each person we come in contact with: to the air conditioner salesman who comes to our house, to the man who delivers firewood? (Witnessing has to be done under God's direction, however, and much harm can be done by rushing ahead of God.)

A friend of the family who works in the receiving department of a large drugstore was blessed when a deliveryman arrived one day praising the Lord. They both had a glorious time sharing what the Lord was doing in their lives. So, wherever we are, that is our point of contact to share Jesus — even at the back door of a drug store.

I asked Ed to sum up faithfulness in one sentence. He said that to him, faithfulness is the ability to persevere and believe. We can never please God without faith, without depending on Him (see Hebrews 11:6).

God tells us in Isaiah 45:7, "... *I send good times and bad* ..." Faithfulness is to believe even when things go wrong and to have faith when everything looks bleak.

Do you recall when the disciples were in the boat doing exactly what Jesus told them to do — to come to Him. They were right in the center of God's will when the storms came and the waves became turbulent. We may be in the dead center of God's will also — yet we may be experiencing trials and tribulations.

When we're in a raging storm, we must reach out to Jesus, not friends or family, but Jesus. We must remember also — just because someone may be having problems, doesn't necessarily mean he is not doing God's will.

Some people find it hard to have faith in anything or to be faithful to anyone. Perhaps they could not trust their parents. They may have been deserted, and they grew up with feelings of suspicion and the inability to trust or to have faith.

If a dad always promised his son that he would take him fishing, to the ball game, or to the circus, making elaborate plans and then consistently breaking his promises at the last minute, the son may grow up not being able to trust or to have faith in anyone. His emotional make-up will be such that he finds it difficult to be dependable or to be faithful, himself. He will find it difficult to trust or to be trustworthy.

But that can be changed. God can change those negative traits into positive ones. First of all, faith comes by hearing, and hearing by the Word of God (see Romans 10:17). So stay in God's Word to build up your faith. Pray without ceasing to become spiritually strong. Occasionally, a person will say, "I accepted Jesus as my Savior, I was filled with the Spirit, and all I've had are trials and troubles — I thought all my problems would leave." Peter said, *"These trials are only to test your faith, to see whether or not it is strong and pure. It is being tested as fire tests gold and purifies it — and your faith is far more precious to God than mere gold; so if your faith remains strong . . . it will bring you much praise and glory and honor on the day of his return" (I Peter 1:7).*

If you have trouble being faithful, perhaps you have been agreeing to do more things than you possibly can do. Pray before you agree to do something: "Lord, is this what You want me to do?" If you get the "go ahead" from the Lord, then be "faithful" and do it. Make certain your priorities are straight. Line up everything you do with God's Word. Christians, of all people, need to be honest, dependable, faithful, and trustworthy. James admonished us with *". . . what's the use of saying that you have faith and are Christians if you aren't proving it by helping others? . . . Faith that doesn't show itself by good works is no faith at all – it is dead and useless" (James 2:14,17).*

Don't excuse your inability to be faithful by saying that you were not taught to be faithful. God is our teacher, and He is constantly admonishing us to be faithful. Replace all negative thoughts with positive ones. Tell yourself, "Yes, I know God wants me to be faithful. Yes, I will be faithful, whether it is in my relationship to God, my family, church, friends, or business."

Charles Spurgeon was quoted as saying, "Little faith will bring your soul to heaven; great faith will bring heaven to your soul."

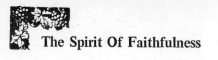

PRAYER FOR FAITHFULNESS

Dear Lord, I want to be called a faithful servant. I want to be dependable. Lord, I want to have faith. Please set me free from any negative force that would make me doubt or to waver. Oh, God, help me to be trustworthy and to trust You. Help me to be faithful.

If I was not taught faithfulness, if I was disappointed and betrayed time after time, help me to forgive, and Lord, please heal those painful memories. My prayer is that You will fill me with faith. Give me a gift of faith. And then, Lord, help me to be filled with the fruit of faithfulness to You, to my mate, to my family and friends. In Jesus' name I pray. Amen.

SCRIPTURES ON FAITHFULNESS

Proverbs 28:20 KJV *"A faithful man shall abound with blessings . . ."*

I Corinthians 4:2 KJV *"Moreover, it is required in stewards, that a man be found faithful."*

Revelation 2:10 KJV *". . . Be thou faithful unto death, and I will give thee a crown of life."*

I Timothy 1:12 *"How thankful I am to Christ Jesus our Lord for choosing me as one of his messengers, and giving me the strength to be faithful to him . . ."*

Matthew 24:45-47 *"Are you a wise and faithful servant of the Lord? Have I given you the task of managing my household, to feed my children day by day? Blessings on you if I return and find you faithfully doing your work. I will put such faithful ones in charge of everything I own!"*

Matthew 25:23 *" 'Good work,' his master said. 'You are a good and faithful servant. You have been faithful over this small amount, so now I will give you much more.' "*

Luke 16:10 KJV *"He that is faithful in that which is least is faithful also in much: and he that is unjust in the least is unjust also in much."*

9

THE FRUIT OF GENTLENESS

 here is some false teaching on submission floating around. But ladies, God did not intend for us to be a submissive doormat, a limp dashrag, a person without a mind. He did intend for us to be the Spirit-filled woman He created us to be. He did create us to be gentle and to exemplify gentleness.

How gentle are we with our children? We *must* be so gentle with our little ones. Sometimes we seem to act as if the children's feelings really don't matter. "They are just kids," we say. Oh, but their feelings do matter. Of course, there has to be discipline, but we can discipline in love. Disciplining in anger, harshness, and gruffness can cause such deep, emotional wounds. Do we listen as they share their inner-most thoughts?

How gentle are we with our husbands? Just because a man is big, strong, and capable of living in the "concrete jungle" all day, we seem to think he doesn't have a tender spot. Oh, but he does. We must be gentle even with our husbands.

And wives, when your husband breaks down that wall and shares his inner-most thoughts, his dreams and fears, don't ever, ever make light of them or "throw them up to him" at a later time.

A brilliant young man sat in our home heart-broken because his wife had left him and filed for a divorce. The whole crux of the story was that he didn't know how to be gentle.

We asked, "Did you ever help your wife with the new baby?"

"No, that's her job."

"Did you help her with some of the household duties when she was sick?"

"No, my dad never did do that for my mother."

"Did you tell her you appreciated her and loved her?"

"No, and I do very much."

"Did you ever praise her for anything?"

"No, and she was a great cook and mother."

"Were you gentle with her?"

"No, in fact, I struck her."

This young man had been raised in an unloving home where gentleness was not displayed. Gentleness was a sign of weakness to him.

A sign of strength is when a man can be gentle. How precious it is to see a father being gentle with his wife and children. On a flight home recently from a speaking engagement in another state, I was sitting across from a young couple with a new baby. It was that great big,

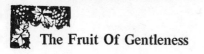

six-foot, husband who held the baby the entire flight. He fed and "burped" the baby. Did I think that young dad was weak or hen-pecked? No, I thought, "Now, there's a man who is so confident of his manliness, he can afford to be gentle."

It seems we hesitate to show gentleness because we are afraid people will think we are weak.

It breaks my heart to see a youngster being rude and making fun of an older person or a deformed person. I believe teasing and calling names is wrong — completely wrong — and should never be tolerated in a family. In fact, Jamie Buckingham in *Risky Living* wrote that we actually place a curse on a child by calling him stupid or dumb-bell.

When a child is unkind to an animal, I wonder what has happened to cause that child to be so hard-hearted and cruel. When a child is unkind to God's four-legged creatures, so often they grow up being unkind to His two-legged creatures as well.

I have heard parents say to their son, "Big boys don't cry." Have you ever been in a situation when a person shows a moment of tenderness (say, when the flag goes by in a parade) and because there was a display of respect and sentimentality, he was teased? Displays of respect and sentimentality are commendable. We could instill no greater trait in our children than to teach them to be gentle (especially our sons). They should be strong, manly, decisive, yes; but *gentle* by all means.

Everyone needs gentleness. Everyone has some type of burden to carry. You don't know what hurt your neighbor has deep inside. Be gentle — so very, very gentle.

Psychologists use the term "pecking syndrome." When a new chicken comes into a flock, it is often pecked to death. Likewise, if a new child comes into an elementary classroom, sometimes the other children will be so unfriendly and so unkind. They will exclude the new student. A wise teacher will encourage her class to include the new student, to be friendly, to be gentle.

When we need to go to the dentist, we pick one who is gentle. Do you remember the nurse in the hospital who so gently changed your bandages? Do you remember how very much you appreciated her gentleness?

Jesus was strong, a man's man; but oh, He was so gentle.

A wife will never love her husband more than when he removes the business mask, takes off the self-sufficient armor that he wears in the business world, and becomes gentle and tender. It takes a strong and secure man to be able to portray gentleness.

You may not have been treated with gentleness as a child. Perhaps you had an overbearing, stern father or a domineering, gruff mother. Perhaps you were taught to be rough and tough — to get "them" — before they get "you." You can be changed! Jesus wants us to be like Him — gentle and kind. Pray this prayer with me, will you? Pray that you will be filled with the fruit of gentleness. We need to remember the saying — Life is *fragile* handle with *prayer.*

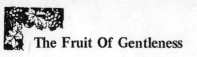

PRAYER FOR THE FRUIT OF GENTLENESS

Lord Jesus, please fill me with the fruit of gentleness. Give me "hearing ears" and "seeing eyes" to be aware when others need an extra touch of gentleness.

When I was treated gruffly and without gentleness as a child, please heal those hurts and fill the void. Help me to show tenderness and gentleness to those around me without compromising Your strength.

Lord, make me so that I won't be concerned about what others think when I am gentle, when I show tenderness, when I shed tears.

Make me like You, Jesus, so gentle. It's in Your name I pray. Amen.

SCRIPTURES ON GENTLENESS

Colossians 3:13 *"Be gentle and ready to forgive; never hold grudges . . ."*

I Peter 3:4 *"Be beautiful inside, in your hearts, with the lasting charm of a gentle and quiet spirit which is so precious to God."*

Proverbs 18:21 KJV *"Death and life are in the power of the tongue . . ."*

Proverbs 15:1 *"A soft answer turns away wrath, but harsh words cause quarrels."*

James 1:26 *"Anyone who says he is a Christian but doesn't control his sharp tongue is just fooling himself, and his religion isn't worth much."*

I Thessalonians 5:14 *". . . take tender care of those who are weak . . ."*

Psalm 18:35 *". . . Your right hand, O Lord, supports me; your gentleness has made me great."*

Titus 3:2 *"They must not speak evil of anyone, nor quarrel, but be gentle and truly courteous to all."*

II Timothy 2:24 *"God's people must not be quarrelsome; they must be gentle, patient teachers of those who are wrong."*

10

THE FRUIT OF SELF-CONTROL

aul deals with the problem of self-control in Romans 7:19 where he said, *"When I want to do good, I don't; and when I try not to do wrong, I do it anyway."* Praise the Lord that He does not give up on us. He keeps on loving us, teaching us, chastening us, molding us, picking us up when we fall, helping us — even when we've lost self-control.

God wants us to have self-control in all areas of our life, including:

our eating
our emotions
our habits
our finances
our spiritual walk.

Have you ever lost your self-control? Has anger ever overcome you to a point of rage? Have you heard your voice lashing out and you asked yourself, "Am I really saying those things?"

There are those who will admit, "Yes, I have a temper just like my dad. I can't control it."

"I have a weight problem just like my mom. I can't control my appetite. She craved chocolates, too."

The alcoholic says, "I just had to have one more drink."

The chain smoker cannot control the desire to smoke.

The compulsive gambler loses control. He is always going-to-win-on-the-next-chance.

The suburban housewife says to her irate husband, "Honey, I just couldn't control myself. I just had to buy all those clothes today." (And some men are just as bad about over-spending as women.)

The murderer behind bars says, "I couldn't control myself. I went into a rage and I killed someone."

The promiscuous teen-ager says, "I couldn't control my emotions. Now I'm pregnant."

The teen-age boy says, "I lost control of my thinking, and I gave in to the gang and smoked pot. I'm hooked on it now."

Self-control.

If God lives in us, if we allow Him to be in control, if we give our wills to Him, then He controls those emotions of ours. But if we try to handle it ourselves without God, it gives Satan a chance at the "controls" of our life and emotions.

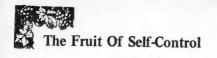
God will not come in and override our wills. But when we invite Him to take control, He will take that irrational behavior and make us into the person He wants us to be.

Lack of self-control is contagious to a degree. If the husband's boss loses his temper and self-control and yells at the husband, "Why isn't this work finished?" and insinuates, "Either shape up or ship out;" the husband may come home with his emotions out of control. He gripes at the wife because the house isn't clean and dinner isn't ready.

If the wife doesn't have self-control, she will become upset and will, in turn, yell at the child, lashing out at him, "Why didn't you take the garbage out?" or, "Must I always tell you to clean your feet before you come into the house?" Then, in utter frustration, she yells, "Get outside 'til dinner is ready."

The child who is trying to learn from Mother and Dad the art of self-control goes outside hurt and angry and kicks the dog and pushes his baby brother.

Self-control.

We never know how much or little self-control we have until we are tempted or tested. A friend's husband suffered from a terminal illness for two years in the depths of agony and pain. Moment by moment she watched him suffer and die. They were beautiful Christians who really walked in the Spirit. We can't understand God's way. But to those watching from the side, she practiced a living example of self-control in unbearable circumstances. Of course, she experienced all the emotions of one going through such a trial, but she was in control of her emotions. She didn't let them control her.

One of the most damaging areas and the most misused is our tongue. Lack of control of our words results in anger, gossip, criticism, or negative confession. We have life and death in our mouth. Reputations have been destroyed, friendships broken, because of a slip of the tongue. Discouraged people have gone on to success because someone offered encouragement and hope – just with the kind words from their mouth.

The first few seconds after an incident happens that might cause us to lose our self-control is the time to bind Satan in the name of Jesus and to silently pray in the Spirit, turn, and walk away. A strong person turns and walks away instead of giving in to that moment of anger, etc. A strong person with self-control will not repeat that juicy little tidbit of gossip.

Occasionally we have heard in prayer groups a prayer request that really was more than a prayer request. It was a chance for someone to share a little "tainted" information disguised as a "compassionate" prayer request.

I heard an evangelist share this documented story. He said the episode involved a preacher in a small town in a western state. It seems the preacher was seen by the town gossip leaving the bus station with a young shapely blond on his arm. The gossip didn't wait until she got home; she called from the bus station and started the rumor that their pastor had another woman.

By nightfall, the story was all over town. At nine o'clock that night, the head elder came to the pastor's

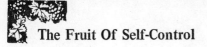
door and told him there was a group of people asking for his resignation. He had been seen with a young blonde. The stunned pastor said, "I'll see you in church in the morning."

Sunday morning, the church was packed. Before the pastor started his sermon, he said, "There is a rumor going around that I have been seen about town with a young woman. It is no rumor. It's the truth, and I want you to meet that young lady. I want you to meet my younger sister that I haven't seen in years."

The gossip stood up and cried out, "Oh, Pastor, I started that rumor. Will you forgive me?"

The pastor said, "Yes, on one condition." He pulled out a feather pillow from under the pulpit. "My son is going to carry this to the roof and rip it apart and let all the feathers float away. When you have picked up all the feathers and brought them back to me, I'll forgive you."

Of course, we're to forgive unconditionally, without "if clauses." But the truth is, gossip, once started is almost impossible to stop. This true story reminds us to guard our tongues, to watch exaggeration, to practice self-control in our minds and emotions as well as our habits.

PRAYER FOR SELF-CONTROL

Dear God, You know me better than I do. You know all my weaknesses and all my flaws. Thank You for loving me just the way I am. Will You please take control of my life. Will You fill me with Your fruit of self-control.

Lord, make me strong enough to resist Satan. Please take away the desires that are not of You (name what it is: the desire to drink, smoke, gamble, over-spend, gossip, exaggerate, over-eat). Make me strong in You, Lord. It is in the name of Jesus I pray. Amen.

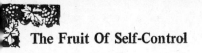

SCRIPTURES ON SELF-CONTROL

James 3:2 *"If anyone can control his tongue, it proves that he has perfect control over himself in every other way."*

Proverbs 13:3 *"Self-control means controlling the tongue ..."*

Proverbs 10:19 *"Don't talk so much. You keep putting your foot in your mouth. Be sensible and turn off the flow."*

Philippians 2:14 *"In everything you do, stay away from complaining and arguing ..."*

Ephesians 4:26 *"... Don't let the sun go down with you still angry ..."*

James 1:19 *"Dear brothers, don't ever forget that it is best to listen much, speak little, and not become angry ..."*

James 1:26 *"Anyone who says he is a Christian but doesn't control his sharp tongue is just fooling himself, and his religion isn't worth much."*

Proverbs 25:28 KJV *"He that hath no rule over his own spirit is like a city that is broken down, and without walls."*

EPILOGUE

 here is no place on earth where we need to practice the fruit of the Spirit more than in our own homes, before and with our children. We have such a responsibility as parents to exemplify the fruit of the Spirit. Children learn Christianity in action by watching Mother and Dad.

Children Learn What They Live
by Dorothy Law Nolte

May 1954

If a child lives with criticism — he learns to condemn.
If a child lives with hostility — he learns to fight.
If a child lives with fear — he learns to be apprehensive.
If a child lives with pity — he learns to feel sorry for himself.
If a child lives with ridicule — he learns to be shy.
If a child lives with jealousy — he learns what envy is.
If a child lives with shame — he learns to feel guilty.
If a child lives with encouragement — he learns to be confident.

If a child lives with tolerance — he learns to be patient.

If a child lives with praise — he learns to be appreciative.

If a child lives with acceptance — he learns to love.

If a child lives with approval — he learns to like himself.

If a child lives with recognition — he learns it is good to have a goal.

If a child lives with sharing — he learns about generosity.

If a child lives with honesty and fairness — he learns what truth and justice are.

If a child lives with security — he learns to have faith in himself and those about him.

If a child lives with friendliness — he learns that the world is a nice place in which to live.

If you live with serenity — your child will live with peace of mind.*

The only thing more precious than a sweet child filled with the Spirit is a sweet Spirit-filled older person. Someone said, "You can't help what you look like when you're young, but you *are* responsible for what you look like when you're older."

The following poem appeared in our church paper almost eighteen years ago. I cut it out and saved it — I suppose to use in this book. It's really on the fruit of the Spirit; the anonymous author just didn't call it that.

* "Children Learn What They Live," Dr. Dorothy Law Nolte © Living Scrolls. 1972 ` 1975

A PRAYER

Lord, Thou knowest better than I know myself that I am growing older, and will someday be old.

Keep me from getting talkative, and particularly from the fatal habit of thinking that I must say something on every subject and on every occasion.

Release me from craving to try to straighten out everybody's affairs.

Keep my mind free from the recital of endless details — give me wings to get to the point.

I ask for grace enough to listen to the tales of others' pains. Help me to endure them with patience.

But seal my lips on my own aches and pains — they are increasing, and my love of rehearsing them is becoming sweeter as the years go by.

Teach me the glorious lesson that occasionally it is possible that I may be mistaken.

Keep me reasonably sweet; I do not want to be a saint — some of them are so hard to live with — but a sour old person is one of the crowning works of the devil.

Make me thoughtful, but not moody; helpful, but not bossy. With my vast

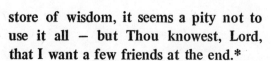

> store of wisdom, it seems a pity not to
> use it all — but Thou knowest, Lord,
> that I want a few friends at the end.*

Whether we're young, old, man, or woman, we, too, can exemplify the fruit of the Spirit. We can be set free from negative emotions. We, too, can be radiant with the love of Jesus. The astronauts spent hours and hours training before they went to the moon. Should we do any less than spend hours praying, poring over God's Word before we take those giant (or tiny) steps for God?

Exemplifying the fruit of the Spirit doesn't just happen. It requires work. Straight A's in school require much effort. Most pianists have to practice untold hours to be able to play Bach or Chopin without flaws. Likewise, we will have to "work" at our vineyard to produce good fruit.

Good fruit only comes from strong, healthy vines and trees. Good spiritual fruit only comes from a spiritual vineyard well-tended. We tend our spiritual vineyards by:

1. staying in God's Word, reading the Bible every day,
2. staying in a Spirit-filled fellowship,
3. constantly pruning back bad attitudes, cutting off weak branches (negative emotions) by being aware of diseased places (hurt feelings) and allowing God to cleanse those places with the oil of the Holy Spirit,
4. daily forgiving anyone who has hurt us in any way,

 *Author unknown.

5. praying in the Spirit daily (praying without ceasing). Earthly vines grow with water, sunshine, and cultivation. We become strong spiritually by praying in the Spirit.

If you are having trouble with negative emotions, and after praying by yourself and doing all the things you know to do, you still don't have victory, perhaps you need someone to agree with you in prayer. The Bible says in Matthew 18:19, "... *if two of you agree down here on earth concerning anything you ask for, my Father in heaven will do it for you.*"

You may need someone to pray with you using the authority he has in Jesus to bind Satan from you, to help you renounce all the negative forces that are hindering your spiritual growth. You may need the prayer for healing of memories,* asking the Lord Jesus to heal the wounds that are keeping you from showing love, having peace and joy, from practicing self-control, and the other fruit of the Spirit.

Don't become discouraged if it seems you will never have all the fruit of the Spirit at one time. Just keep striving. Keep praying and praising. And just listen; someone may say to you, "I can tell whose child you are. You look just like your daddy." Listen very closely. You may hear the Lord saying, "Well done, My good and faithful servant."

God's Word admonishes and reminds us, *"You didn't choose me! I chose you! I appointed you to go and produce lovely fruit always..." (John 15:16).*

Let's go and produce lovely fruit —
Shall We?

*See Chapter VII in *Inner Healing Through Healing of Memories* for prayer for healing of memories.